THE NATURAL HAND
& THE ART OF PRACTICING

Vol. I
The Keyboard Instruments

by Uli Geissendoerfer

Cover Design by Sarah Samira Yancey

www.innovativeinkpublishing.com
Send all inquiries to:
4050 Westmark Drive
Dubuque, IA 52004-1840

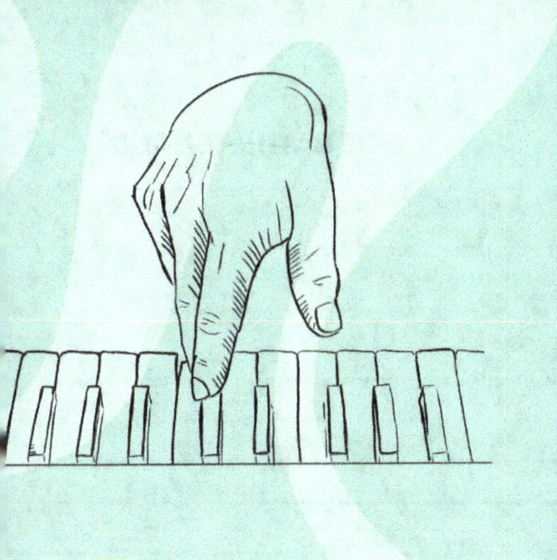

Contents

Part I—The Natural Hand for Piano and Keyboard Instruments

CHAPTER I—THE BASIC CONCEPTS 1

CHAPTER II—TONE PRODUCTION 7

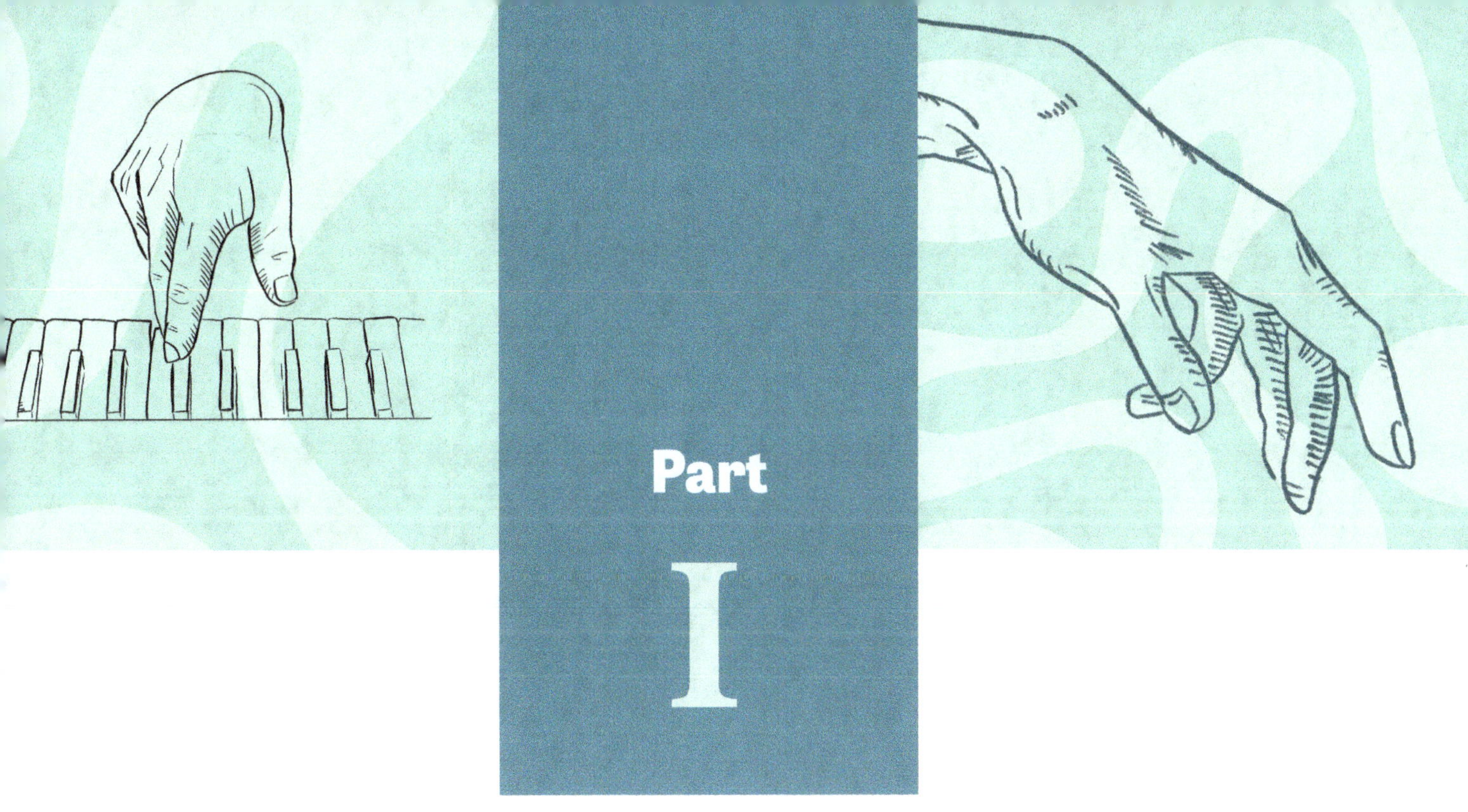

Part

I

The Natural Hand for Piano and Keyboard Instruments

Introduction

Greetings and salutations to all readers. The concept of *The Natural Hand* was developed over the past several decades but came to real fruition during the past 12 years of my teaching at UNLV. Much inspiration came from studying with the late Mike Longo. His insights opened doors to my own understanding of technique, musicianship, jazz, and music in general. I feel very fortunate to have worked with Mike.[1] I also realized when talking to other instrumentalists, and not pianists, about my approach, that everyone agreed and had similar or comparable views and approaches. However, there seemed to be no book, compendium, or the like available focusing on this approach, and I was encouraged and cheered on by all to put one together. So here is the first volume. I encourage all readers to actively reflect upon the method and please reach out to me with your comments and own observations. The goal is to have an effortless approach to playing instruments and to help any player, whether starting out or already playing for some time.

While teaching, especially at the college level, I realized that most students were held back by a lack of physiological understanding or, in other words, bad technique. Mind you, there's a plethora of issues that can hold one back. Problems such as inaccurate hearing, lack of focus, lack of discipline, lack of social skills, and lack of self-confidence (for a discussion of these, see chapter 9, Part II) come to mind. All of these aspects I will eventually talk about, but the biggest and first concern should be a positive and effortless approach to your instrument. After all, music is a physical manifestation. To put it simply, if you can't feel it in your body, you will have a hard time to manifesting it on your instrument. This is where *The Natural Hand's* approach starts.

In this first volume, I show the general principles that are applicable to all instruments and then we will zoom into piano technique. In later volumes, I will focus on the other instrument groups: strings, winds, drums and percussion, and voice, all with the help of master players and educators discussing their basic approaches and applications. I truly believe, however, that everyone, regardless of the instrument, will get something out of this first volume.

I am indebted to all my teachers, in chronological order—Frau Diehl, Herr Professor Rottler, Maestro Milos Radosevic, Dr. Steven Harlos, Dan Haerle, Jack Peterson, Bert Ligon, Chu Chen, Berthe Odnoposoff, Harold Danko, Maestro Chucho Valdés, Guru Mike Longo, and Dave Loeb. All of you showed me some invaluable stuff. Often, I was not the most diligent and best student, but I always had my radar wide open to learn about the individual, and the things in between the notes: their energy, their impetus and intent, the way they held themselves, the way they talked about music and styles, their peers and their masters. I observed the way they greet you and are greeted by others and their replies and the way they contemplate and carefully formulate answers and sometimes not answer, but just act. And this all reflects in their playing and sound![2]

Possibly even more grateful I am to all my students throughout the years. You opened my eyes, and your problems were my shining light. May all of you continue to make me proud and inspire me.

There is so much to to learn, study, and figure out that it is almost overwhelming, but it starts with a clear approach to your instrument. This is the reason for this book and series, which focuses primarily on the physical approach to one's instrument and the approach to practicing. I did not present a lot of exercises, as these can be readily found in literature everywhere. You will find in Appendix III a list of great technical compendiums. I sometimes forget, as I pick through them to find just the one good exercise that is most suitable for the given student at that time, that all of them represent a lot of studying and reflecting upon the mastery of piano. So much is to be found even in the smallest etude. Often, what you seek will guide you. And never forget, you are your own best teacher. Any teacher is merely a guide to point out the way. How to actually accomplish anything is up to you. This is what prompted the second part of this book.

A note on how to use this book: There's no need to read it from beginning to end or in any specific order besides the basic approach to the natural hand. Especially in the second part just pick one page or idea and run with it. Feel free to jump around. More than anything, I like to spike the reader's curiosity and stimulate great practicing and dazzling musical outcomes.

---

[1]Mike's vast understanding of music and its inner workings came from working with Dizzy Gillespie for some 25 years and his early studies with Oscar Peterson, arguably the man with the golden touch. Peterson's fluidity and pearly sound are recognizable amid a hundred players, and this is where we start. How do you produce such a sound? How to be so lose yet so in control of phrasing and groove? In all piano playing, the one figure that is pivotal and the link to modern times is Franz Liszt. Arguably one of the most brilliant musicians ever, his technique has had no equal, but his musical legacy and teaching has left a trail still gleaming bright, and would you know Oscar Peterson stands in this tradition through his teacher, Paul De Marky, who was a student of Stephan Thomán's in Budapest, himself a pupil of Liszt's.

[2]An aside—I probably learned as much from Cannonball Adderley's introductions and announcements of tunes, as from his playing. His diction, swagger, and flow indelibly showed me, the foreigner then, another very important aspect of jazz—the attitude toward the music, our peers, and the audience.

Things to Ponder

Sergei Rachmaninov—not only composer of the most amazing romantic piano music (*The Seven Year Itch* anyone?) but also a pianist with an extraordinary technique—said:

Music is enough for a lifetime, but one lifetime is not enough for music!

Ludwig van Beethoven is arguably the most contemporary-sounding of all classical composers and is the one with largest audience appeal to this day. He was also the first freelance composer, not bound to any financial or employment allegiance—he wrote from his heart to all humanity.

To play a wrong note is unimportant, to play without feeling, unforgivable!

Which means, to not be physically involved, is not acceptable! How to be maximally involved is by making your instrument an extension of your own physique!

Bill Evans—The brilliant jazz pianist and composer who created a unique sound and forged the way for great artists like Lyle Mays and Keith Jarrett.

He reflects on how his finger position had changed over the years:

"When I was younger, I played with flat fingers … when we possess a lot of vitality and we have a lot of energy, this method of playing permits you to use your energy effectively. As I matured technically, I noticed that my fingers curled when I played. It is a more natural position which was used by Mozart, Haydn and especially Bach." (Interview with François Postif, Les Grandes Interviews de Jazz Hot, 1989)

"Knowing the problem is 90% of solving it!"

Dick Hyman, one of the most prolific jazz pianists, is known for his brilliant quotes:

"The solution to nervousness is to practice enough."

"Almost anything you practice helps."

"When I grew up, Jazz was the music of the streets—it wasn't taught."

Lenni Tristano is known for his great Bebop playing and being the founder of the first Jazz School, devoting much of his life to teaching jazz and creating a legacy with students like Wayne March and Lee Konitz:

"The Hippest thing you can do, is not to play at all, just listen!"

"The jazz musicians' function is to feel!"

"It's not instant composing; it's not following any kind of formula. All you do is, hear music in your head and reproduce it!"

The best student is the one who does not want to impress the teacher, especially with words.

Old universal wisdom

Moments of sheer joy, where the listener is transported—that's what we want to create!

Volker Barber, composer (after a concert by the author which he attended)

"Man muss noch Chaos in sich haben, um einen tanzenden Stern gebären zu können."

(You must still have chaos within you to give birth to a dancing star.)"

Friedrich Nietzsche, *Thus Spoke Zarathustra*

Any tension before the finger tip severs the connection between the music and the soul, and the wrist is often the culprit!

Claudio Arrau

Music Improvisation: just like in reading, when we subject ourselves to the author's language and flow, which sucks us in and transports us into a different place and time.

Anonymous

"If you take care of the music, it will take care of you!"

Larry Willis (Roy Hargrove recounted Larry telling him this)

And maybe one of the most important nuggets of wisdom by **Jim Riggs**, former director of the 2 o'clock Lab Band at UNT:

Performing music is the obvious display of the ability to concentrate!

The following three concepts are the most important building blocks. Keep these in mind when you approach your instrument:

> The Natural Hand Position
>
> Solid First Knuckle
>
> Ring of Energy

As much as this first book is a manual on how to approach the piano, it is also a general way of checking in with your body and physique. The principles outlined can be applied to basically all instruments (and many physical activities as well). Remember, if you can't feel it, you'll have a hard time manifesting it.

Now let's see how to get there.

For any comments about the method and questions about specific repertoire (songs or classical pieces) and how to apply the natural hand to it, please contact me at:

the.natural.hand.uli@gmail.com

I

The Basic Concepts

1. CONCEPT: The Natural Hand Position

Let's get started!

Kindly stand up and stand straight. Let your arms droop. You should be relaxed yet standing tall.

Step 1—Let us simply look at your hands. Please only observe your hands but do not move them. The way they hang down is their natural state. There is a natural curvature to them resulting from the equilibrium between the muscles that bend and stretch the fingers.

Step 2—Please move your fingers. Observe the ease of movement.

Step 3—Let's look at where the muscles that move your fingers are situated. You find them right here in your forearm. The substantial muscles in your hand are the group of muscles that belong to the thumb (six are in the hand, three are in the forearm), and the pinky muscles.

Step 4—Please reflect on their placement. If all the muscles were indeed in your hand, your hands would be about twice the size without much ability for subtle movements and control and simply a big blob of muscles.

Step 5—So how does the arm work? Look at the graphic, and you'll see the muscles and the fingers. They are connected by tendons that go through the *Carpel Tunnel*, which is the band around your wrist. In actuality, it is a band of ligaments that doesn't like to be stressed in the wrong way, or you are facing symptoms of carpel tunnel syndrome and/or tendinitis, which we'll get to later.

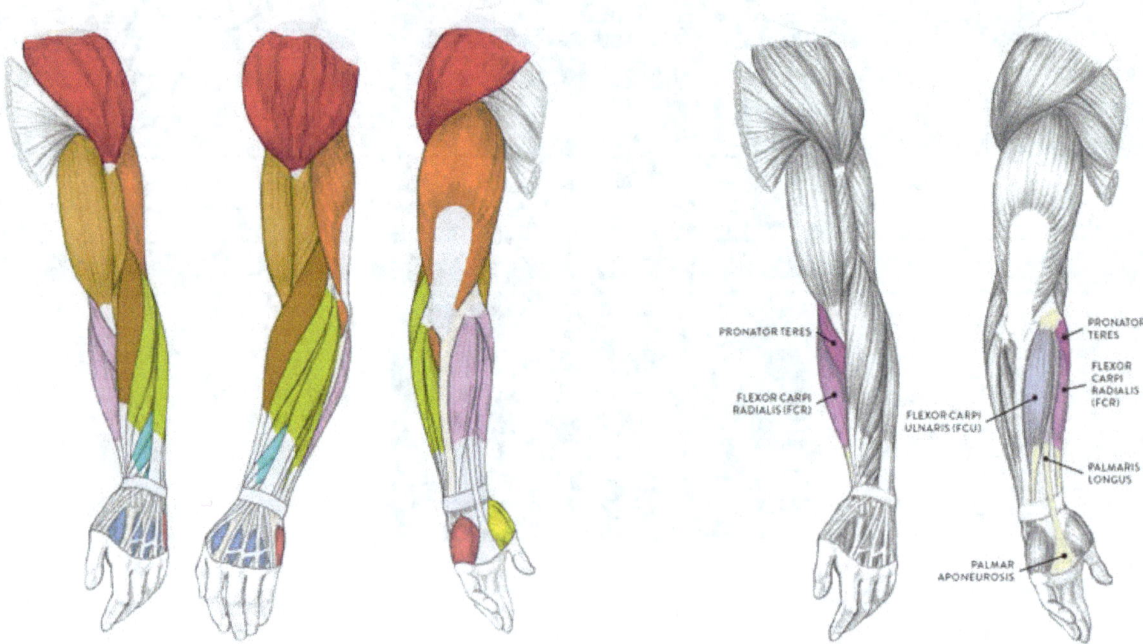

The two images above are taken from the brilliant Doctorlib website. You can see many more interesting pictures and explanations about the hand movement there: https://doctorlib.info/anatomy/classic-human-anatomy-motion/7.html

Step 6—Ligaments are the ones that carry the energy to the tip of our fingers. Because of this, we need to keep the last knuckle solid! Otherwise, all that beautiful energy gets absorbed and does not yield us proper control of the key and accuracy of the sound. Below, you see the ligaments and how they are connected.

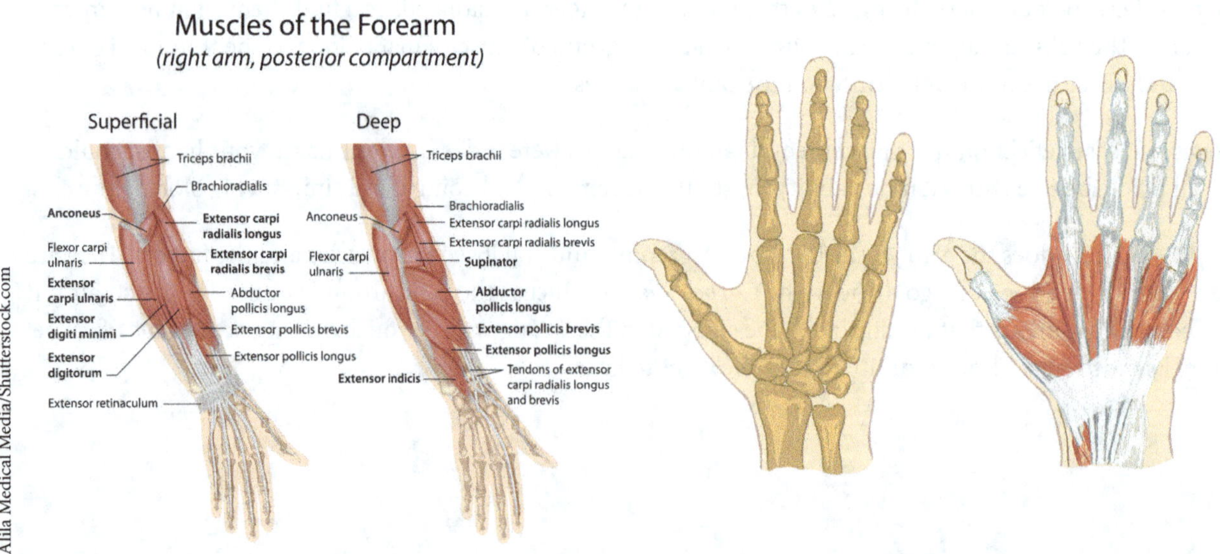

Before you watch the video, take a moment and find all the muscles and ligaments pictured in your hands. Push up your shirt or garment and wiggle your fingers to see your muscles move.

Introduction

2. CONCEPT: Easy Wrist

Step 7—Now please observe the wrist.

The wrist is a miracle of design, capable of twisting and turning, even at the same time. You may call it the scaffolding to your hand. It enables your hands' movements and the placement of the fingers to do their job—which is, to be little drummers and hammers, translating the muscles' force into harmonious action and, ultimately, sound.

Therefore, we need to keep the wrist loose most of the time. View it as a conduit that translates movement and enables the fingers to be perfectly placed, as our fingers are rather limited in movement. The only digit with a lot of reach is the thumb. It has reach and grace and helps us play scales—arpeggios and the like.

3. CONCEPT: Arm Position and Movement

.*Step 8*—Please observe the movement of the hands when we raise them. The arms naturally curve outward when raised, creating a little circle. This in turn provides the arms and the chest the freedom to move.

Now the arm movement when we traverse the keyboard. Two points govern the motion. Imagine strings attached on your wrist and your elbow. The arms' movement is directed from there and enables the fingers or hammers to be always in the best and easiest and, thus, comfortable position.

arm movement

4. CONCEPT: Solid Knuckle

Now that we have seen the movement of the arms and the muscles, the most important concept is the solid first knuckle. I touched on it before; this is a universal concept and applies to almost anything. We only have control, if the last part of the control and action chain is solid. The final joint in the finger needs all the attention we can muster. See the difference when you strike the key with a soft and a strong knuckle. In the video below, you see how a soft knuckle almost works as a shock absorber. Do observe that difference in touch and sound when I play like this (strong knuckle) and like that (soft knuckle). While I'll leave you with this thought for a moment, try it out for yourself.

knuckle

So, what's next? Let's go to the piano.

5. CONCEPT: Ring of Energy

I want to introduce you to this powerful concept. And it is a concept that is common to all instruments. You and your instrument are to be one; ideally you play and express the intent of the music as soon as it forms in your mind and body. For that, a relaxed yet firm posture is key.

How and where that balance aligns is personal and even differs from instrument to instrument. I feel slightly different when I play piano or Rhodes, Hammond or synth (not to mention Harpsichord and church organ). Mostly it is the sound that makes a difference and makes me play accordingly. As many of you will know, things that work on a piano do not necessarily sound good on a Rhodes, where fewer notes are more effective due to the thicker sound—same for the Hammond. Nonetheless, the basic alignment and concepts are identical.

For a clearer visual, please check out the two videos below:

position at piano

Step 1—Let your arms dangle at ease.

Step 2—Now move them to atop the keyboard. Please observe the positioning of your arms. Ideally, you form a ring of energy with your piano. The elbows are out, the shoulder muscles support the whole arm, wrists are loose and free, and the fingers can move without obstacle. It's easy, isn't it? If it's not, it's probably because you have to think a lot to maintain a relaxed state. No worries, it may take time, but not a whole lot.

sitting

Step 3—In order to properly sit and support our body we need to focus on the need of the body in play. The need is that we have to be able to move freely at all times.

A. Use your seat bones and not your thighs to support you. Ideally, you can do this where your feet and hands are supported by your seat and buttocks.

B. Align your navel with middle "c" (that stays the same with keyboards and synths regardless of notes, for example, 88, 85, 76, 73, 61 [five octaves are most common], or 49). We need to be aware of our physical center and torso pivot.

C. Keep about a forearm-length distance; ideally you can touch your elbows in front of your belly (given a trim figure).

D. Your feet are firmly planted here and here or here and here or here and here or really wherever you need them. The key is to plant them firmly wherever they feel comfortable to you. Here jazz and classical often differ in that in jazz and many contemporary styles use very little pedal, as the music is more percussive and requires rhythmic definition. Often the foot is used to keep time and inner rhythmic balance. My preferred placement for the right foot on a piano and grand is bent to the right and only half on top of the pedal. When playing keyboards I usually have the pedal fairly centered. As and aside, I use the left pedal a lot, where I tend to have more foot on top of it.

feet

E. Upper body: Your arms and wrists are loose, but firm. Your shoulder is solid, carrying the weight and holding the play apparatus, your arm.

F. Use of pedal: This deserves a whole chapter. For the moment it shall suffice to say that the less pedal you use, the clearer and accurate and ultimately better your sound is. Full pedal is used sparingly, but to great effect and power. When you press the pedal, you activate all strings to sympathetic string movement and sounding, which literally opens up all notes to become part of your sound.

Let's just play do re mi fa so (c-d-e-f-g). Do so again, and check with your left hand and your right wrist. Do you feel tension while you play? If not, congratulations, but kindly check twice. Most people experience tension in the wrist, which is not so good, as it slows you down and actually decreases your accuracy. How come? It's simply friction—like driving a car with a pulled handbrake. The less you have, the quicker you can move. In the next chapter, I'll explain the way to a very relaxed and natural touch.

6. Research—Homework

Homework is checking out famous pianists at work.

Go to concerts and go online and watch how they use their physique to manifest the music. How do they sit, how do they phrase, with the arm, with the body, and what about their heads and mimicry?

Turn off the sound. Can you still imagine their playing? How much does the visual transport the message?

Siemaszko Zbysko

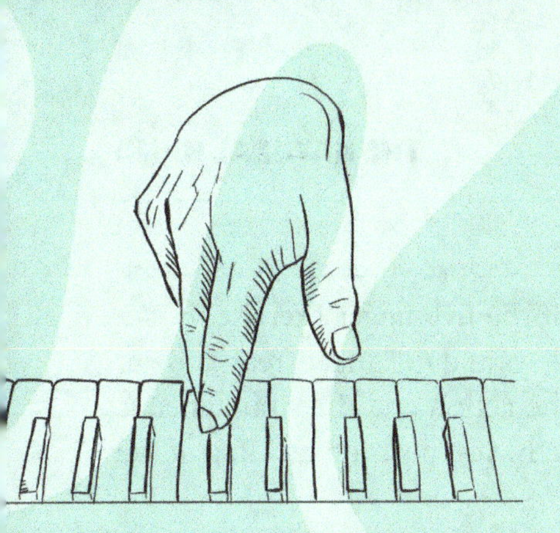

II

Tone Production

This is a short interview with my student Micah Smith. He is a bright young man and immensely talented. Keep your ears out for him.

Micah intro

1. CONCEPT: Finger versus Arm versus Back

Let's look at the difference in tone generation—scale versus chord. A scale is a finger movement aided by the wrist and facilitated by a quick thumb movement. All stays in the forearm. A chord in contrast is facilitated by the back. The fingers assume a shell position of the respective chord and the forearms press it into the key bed.

Okay now in detail. First up, scalar motion.

In order to achieve a scale or any scalar movement, we need to achieve uniformity in touch. How? By taking as much tension away as possible.

Here is very good exercise to get the weight off the arm and keys. I call it the five-finger exercise. It is a whole tone scale from e to c (e, f#, g#, a#, c). Have the wrist dangle above the keys and the fingers reach down, straightening to touch the keys and immediately relax. The rebound of the action and the simultaneous rebound of the muscles will give you a very pearly sound. If it's done correctly, you hear the cackling of the action.

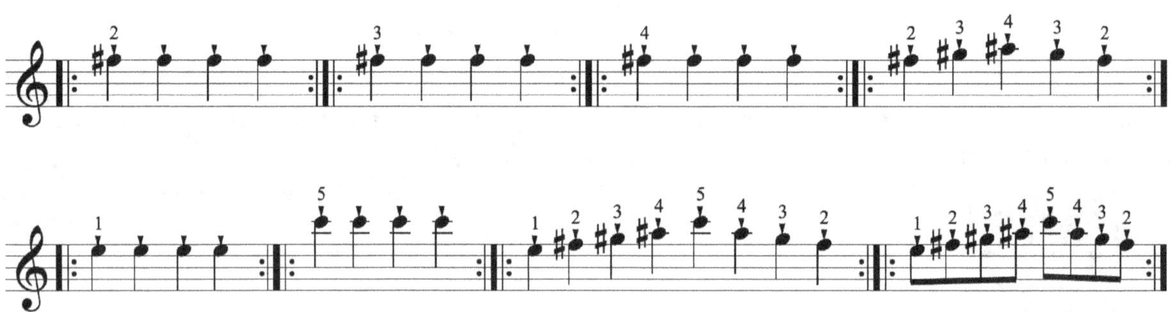

Let's apply this to a tune.

Carl Czerny was one of the most influential pianists and teachers in the first part of the nineteenth century and was himself a student of Beethoven. His music and methods helped herald the age of the (piano) virtuoso.

We can apply the aforementioned touch to his Etude Number 1 of the School of Velocity Op. 299. On my website you can find the whole exercise, but here is the opening.

Finger reaching down excercise - application

Fingers reach down
Arm and wrist are relaxed
Weight is carried by the shoulder
The resulting sound is a light detached short note (pearls)

Carl Czerny
School of Velocity op.299 bk 1

Revised and Adapted by U.G.

We want to play it with the same touch as the five-finger exercise, only this time in the context of a complete scale. It is almost a Staccato, without the sharpness in the attack. The idea is to make maximal use of the recoiling of the finger and the rebounding of the action.

Here is an example of the above with my student Micah:

playing

2. CONCEPT: Importance of Thumb

Now the thumb movement. It is the glue between upward and downward movements.

The thumb has to anticipate the movement (see graphic).

thumb

Secondly, chords.

note versus chord

Concept 3: The Heel—The Groovemaster

How to feel groove? Some of you may simply laugh, and you may simply skip ahead, because you know what it's about. Yet, everyone comes to that fork in the road where you simply cannot play a certain phrase, riff, groove, pattern, juxtaposition, and so on. What to do? Here are my favorite ways of manifesting the groove. I use the word *manifesting*, because you need to feel a phrase in order to play it or, in other words, to physically manifest it.

No matter the style and piece of music we play, whether the meter is:

> even 2/4, 4/4, 12/8, etc.

> odd 3/4, 7/8, 9/8, 11/8, etc.

or a compound meter and groove, all of them have a pulse!

So how do we find and feel the pulse? By manifesting it physically.

The easiest is to use the heel and the heel tap. Why the heel? Tapping with your toes and front foot is somewhat awkward as the toes don't resonate in the rest of your body. The heel does. It's a fairly universal concept used by more musicians than I could recount. When you tap or gently stomp with your heel, it resonates throughout your whole body and makes the groove thus felt internally.

If in contrast you only raise and whip your toes and/or front foot, you won't get the same wholesome experience. Please experiment with it. Although it influences the immediate use of pedal, I don't think it makes much of a difference whether you use the left foot or right foot. With most rhythmical material, pedal is superfluous anyway as it masks the attack and length of the notes. It boils down to personal preference (by the way, I have not seen a pattern that is right-handed versus left-handed, as to who prefers which foot). What's more comfortable and gives you the best grooving feeling you shall use. You are the judge.

The Heel

Playing odd meter music? If it's odd meter, take two bars, half the 8th or quarter note, and you are even again.

Take Five

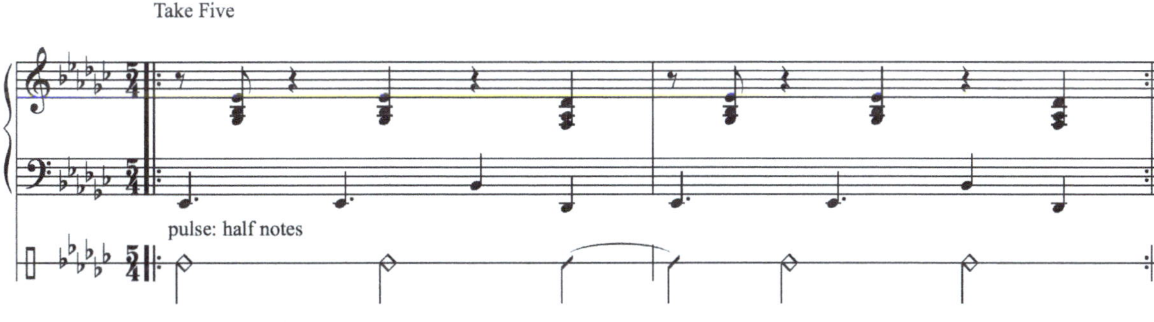

The Extension

Wrestling with a compound meter? Figure out where the pulse lays and which subdivision will unite it. If this sounds a little too easy and simplified—you are right—it is. The key is always the melody. If for example, you happen to play Bulgarian folk music, long compound meters like 25/8 are not uncommon, but it's always melody driven.

Feel free to contact me with specific questions and examples, and we'll work through it and can incorporate them here or on my website.

III

Further Elements

The Foot Placement

Here is where it gets very personal as the foot placement depends on your size and shape.

What is important in this case is you should feel comfortable and experience a sense of stability. I have long legs, so my foot rests in an angle on the sustain pedal as I can't get in under the piano otherwise. Even if you can straighten your leg, several advanced players suggested that you rest your right foot (and somewhat your left foot) at an angle to yield more control and subtleties while pedaling.

What to do with your Feet and Legs

Pedaling

Pedaling for piano—There are so many aspects to pedaling on the piano. It literally is a third hand, allowing us to pedal all aspects of the music. We have:

- **half pedal** and **quarter pedal** where the dampers are barley lifted, and in the case of quarter it still dampens most of the piano. I personally hardly ever use full pedal. Flooring the pedal creates a smudge of a sound that is reserved for special effects.

We can pedal:

a. the melody and phrases
b. the groove (with caution, but you are in stride here, for example)
c. pedal the leaps
d. pedal after the attack—pedal before the attack
e. pedal the phrase—different than the melody

Pedaling is an art that requires much attention.

Two tendencies I always have seen is that, too much pedal is used and that the pedal is pressed too much. Too much equals no control over the sound and its overtones and, very importantly, masks the rhythmic impetus. Very often when playing jazz and other grooving styles, don't use any pedal at all.

Check out sympathetic vibration and half pedal in the video below.

pedaling

The Breath

Generally, it's best to breathe evenly and employ your whole chest.

In Volume 5, when we focus on the voice, I will talk with guest artists extensively about breathing and singing. But for now, I would like to make you aware of the necessity of a good and full breath. These are the elements:

A. The diaphragm
B. Frontal expansion
C. Back expansion

breathing

To be clear the diaphragm is always involved, but it is a matter of focus, in how we employ and to what level we use the front and back. The diaphragm pulls down (see graphic) when inhaling and our torso expands front and back. Please never use a lifting of the shoulders for breathing in. It actually constricts your breathing and equilibrium.

When you practice contemplate how breathing could help you with a phrase. Breathe in and exhale with the phrase following its arch.

When you play and perform don't think about your breath, but do exercises for it daily. Meditation, Tai Chi, Yoga, Pilates, swimming, running, playing tennis, ping pong, and so on—really any form of exercise will work. Friends of mine even lift weights and have no problems playing. This involves a very clear and cautious approach and is best done with a trainer to avoid injuries.

Always remember: "*Mens sane in corpore sano*"—*Healthy mind in healthy body!*

As soon as you feel strain, stop and figure out how to do it better. Having said the above, there are certain things one has to work through, for example, playing a Boogie Woogie left hand. You will cramp up and have to figure out how to relax while keeping it going. However, this is a musical problem. As soon as you have an issue with stretches or angles, please stop.

Inhalation

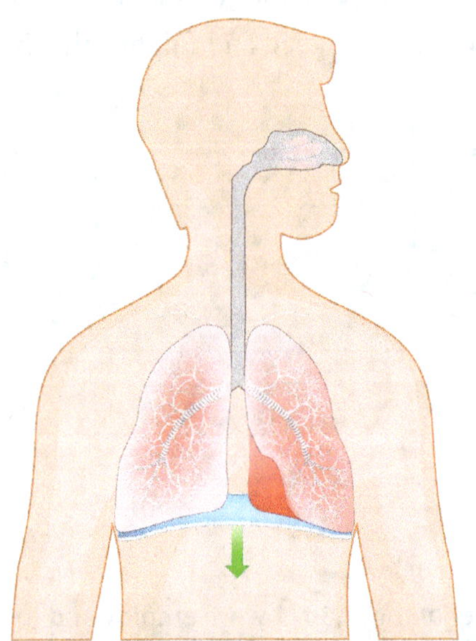

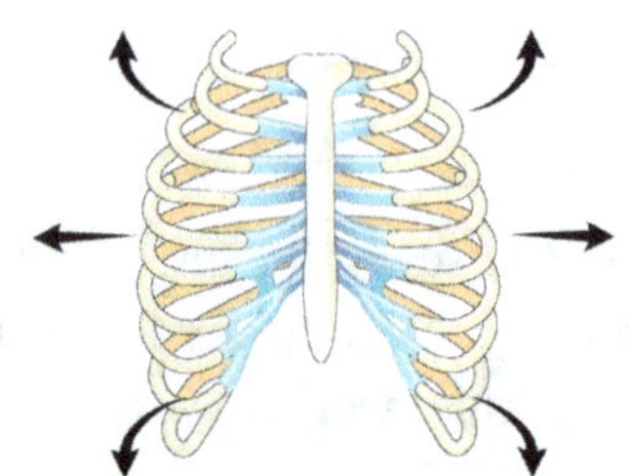

Exhalation

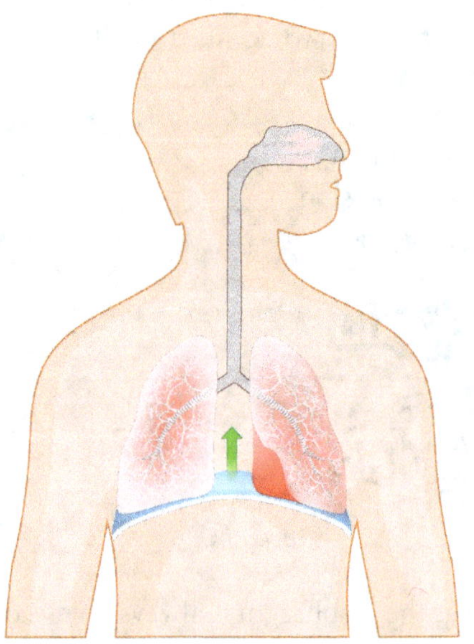

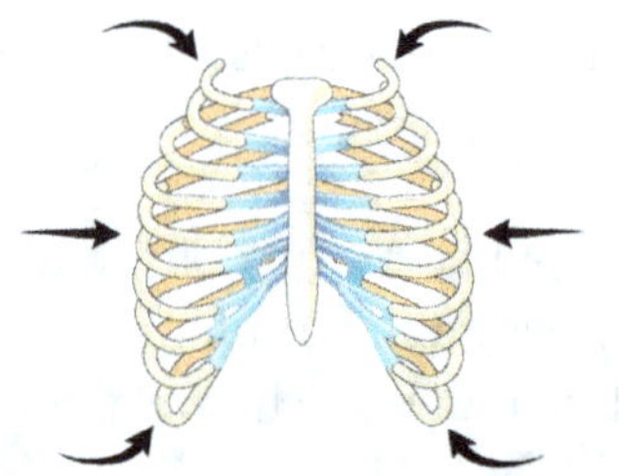

Thought and Focus

One of the biggest problems in performing is focus. So many things can be distracting and make one lose focus. That's why it is necessary to practice in a way that the music enters the subconscious level (see page 19), so no matter the distractions, the music is just there for you to play.

In performing together, the more advanced you become the more you will focus on other players and not so much on yourself. Listen and feel.

In a jazz setting the other musicians and the soloist(s) should always be in focus. One's own playing is more of a reaction. The question to ask for a great outcome is: what is necessary? What fuels the process? How can I positively surprise and change the playing? Often you want to blend in and be supportive rather than be too active. When you improvise the music is always in the air ... it only needs to be played. Find it by listening.

This means we need to do a lot of listening. Not only on the bandstand, but in preparation we need to listen to records (any form of sound playback) where all these concepts are beautifully sonically displayed.

P.S.: A great chapter and discography on how to comp will be found in the most excellent book by Mark Levine—*The Jazz Piano Book.*

Ear and Listening

Music starts with the ear and then come mechanics. This book is mostly about the latter, but I need to write a couple of words about the ear(s) as well.

Musical performance is essentially listening ahead and feeling ahead. The concept here is that performing is continuous anticipation. Thus, in other words, music is anticipatory.

That means your next note is more important than the one you played. Of course, to end any phrase we figure in how we played everything leading up to it. Nonetheless, the concept is that, in any phrase, we are feeling ahead and hearing ahead. We anticipate the coming with physical and emotional preparation. This implies that much of what we do is subconscious (more on that in a moment). And it also implies that we shouldn't judge, for this is an action that shifts the focus away from the inside to the outside and backwards in time to the note already played (see performing).

THE LISTENING CONUNDRUM

One of the most heard statements of advice, especially in jazz, is that one needs to listen ... and listen more and better.

As true as that is, what does that actually mean?

Let me try to pinpoint it. First, we need to know what to listen for!

Music is intensely complex, and there are many aspects that warrant and need our ears attention. Here are building blocks for comprehensive listening.

The groove
The form
The melody
The harmony
The instruments: drums, bass, horns, vocals, guitar, percussion

The emotional development of the tune
The volume (individually and as a whole)
The timbre of the instruments (and the way they expressively change)

Let's listen!

Here is one of jazz's most beloved tracks, *Freddie Freeloader*, from the iconic Miles Davis album—*Kind of Blue*.

Freddie Freeloader

The melody is simple and played with three horns in parallel movement; the piano has short answers to the melody but no comping. The drums play quarter notes on the cymbal and the sidestick on 4. The bass is the most active, almost soloing throughout the head—yes, you read that right, and only with consecutive listening it becomes apparent. The song just oozes tranquility and you're instantly falling into its groove.

Imagine—If you were to be on this session, how would you have played? Can you play along, just playing the fills and hearing everyone? Realize that the piano fills are just the cherry on the icing. The cake is doing well without them. Play through the whole song and entirely focus on every individual instrument. It's an amazing document of restraint and control. Not one note too many, not one note is unnecessary for the whole music, its development, and the architecture of the song.

Are you hearing the form, each beat of the cymbals, the piano, feel the space, the drums riding along? This kind of awareness is what you call listening.

Thus, the process is that we need to be aware of all the different elements listed previously and give them space in our consciousness so that the subconscious can react and direct perfectly. Again, we listen to all these elements; we put them together on the bandstand and let them guide us in our performance. This brings us to the next point—performing.

Performing

A quick reminder of a very important wisdom:
"Performing music is the obvious display of the ability to concentrate." J.Riggs[1]

That means one has to work on the ability to play and the ability to focus.

Where does it start? When one practices! This leads us to the second part of this book—how to practice (just two more pages to go and we're there).

Back to performing. Here are a couple of things that help me to prepare. And mind you, preparation is key.

If you perform written or set material (classical, shows, special concerts, film scores, etc.), know the music inside and out. Play through the music slowly and identify stumbling blocks. Practice these and make little exercises out of them. Turn these stumbling blocks into musical friends. Turn stumbling blocks into skipping stones!

For improvised material, know the music, the repertoire, the players, and rely on the fact that all of the practicing you've done will help you to play beautifully. You don't have to practice or even warm up much at times if you have enough to rely on.

The Judge

One of the biggest problems is the judge. We need to let go of the necessity to judge our playing. The essence should be that we enjoy what we are doing. And if we enjoy it, the audience will do so as well. The energy you radiate is what will influence the listener more than the notes themselves. It provides the authenticity to make music come alive.

The Subconscious

Where do we play from? Which part of our memory is involved when we play? The correct answer is—of course, all of them—but the subconscious is key. This is where memory and active playing reside.

Arguably, many of our tangible and especially not-so-tangible problems stem from a lack of understanding of the subconscious. To me, it's the realm where things actually get done.

The consciousness deals with the here and now, figuring out what event, and which sense to focus on. What piece, of all the information we continuously get bombarded with, necessitates a closer look. It fuels our conversations and helps us with the daily load of improvisations, whether in interaction with another human, an instrument, or any inanimate object.

The subconscious, however, deals with memories and maneuvering the learned. And to it we need to cater when we acquire new knowledge and abilities. Or simpler said—when we practice.

My belief and understanding is that, in order to perform anything, you have to get it to the level of the subconscious—meaning the music is played from the subconscious. How do we get it there? Through diligent and focused practice. And after that practice a very important step has to take place. We must trust ourselves. Only then do you allow the subconscious to work its magic. This necessity to trust can be of course leveraged on any playing situation, and number of players involved. If we don't leverage that trust and respect on everyone else, we and the performance are doomed. Trust is of the essence when performing.

How do we build that trust? As mentioned previously, nothing is better than practice. Remember Dick Hyman's quote: *The solution to nervousness, is to practice enough!*

To know you can rely on what you have acquired and accomplished is essential and very rewarding at the same time. So, let's move on to our next part of the, how to practice.

Here are a couple of questions and ideas about practicing:

Practice away from the instrument

- Actively listen (analyze, feel the form, sing and think along)

Practice with the instrument

- Pacing—How long do I practice before returns diminish?
- Focus—What's my momentary goal?

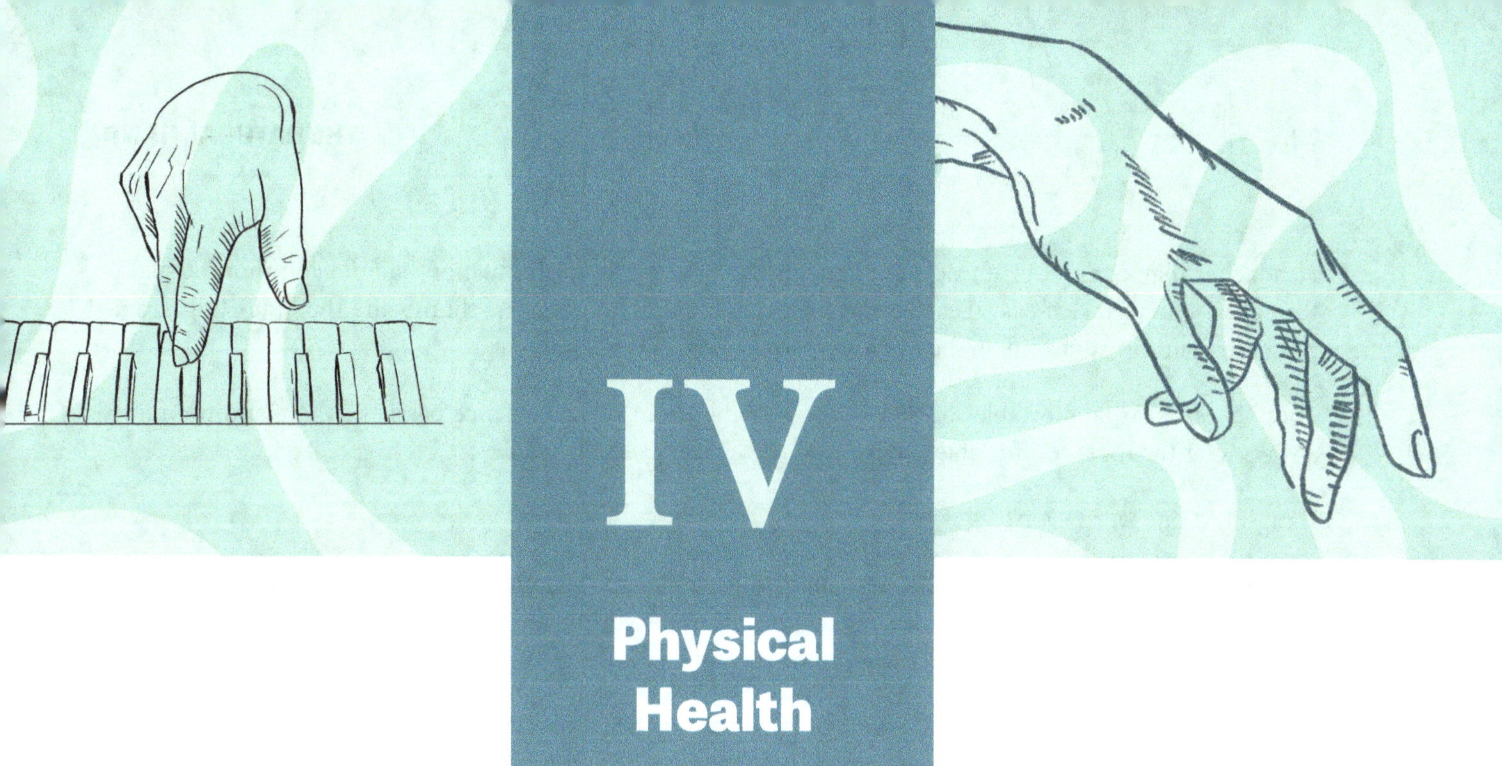

IV

Physical Health

As musicians, no matter whether you're professional or an amateur (and mind you that is not a value statement, just a matter of focus), we face a number of health challenges. The problems range from easily fixable to long term and non-curable. I am not pretending to be a doctor, but will share my experiences about the subject. Health issues and health problems and avoiding them are very much part of The Natural Hand approach.

I like to go back and start with the phrase *healthy mind in healthy body*. Musicians often tend to neglect the necessity of physical balance. This incorporates sleep, diet, emotional balance and physical activity. Ideally one has to become one's own personal life coach.

Let's start with practicing.

As you see in the second part of the book, everything is about a physically most natural and well-timed approach. Tendonitis, Carpal tunnel syndrome, back aches are all avoidable if you keep in mind how your body, your hands, your muscles and ligaments work. Part of learning a musical instrument is to figure out impossible stretches, awkward movements, odd body positions, extremely repetitive movements etc. Do it gently. When something hurts, stop and figure out what the problem is. A cramping up muscle needs stretching and massaging. A hurting tendon needs rest. A back ache comes mostly from a wrong position and needs correcting and strengthening of the lower back muscles or shoulders etc.

Loud is never good for any extended period. You hearing needs a rest, too. And please get yourself musician ear plugs! It's easier to figure out how to play with them than to combat tinnitus etc.

When you're exhausted and you still need to play or practice, then drink water, eat some chocolate or fruit. Simply one banana has saved me more times than I can count.

Headaches may come from muscle cramps, pinched nerves, over stimulation, fatigue and more. Usually, they are a sign to take it easy. Learn to massage key muscles between the thumb and the index finger, and pressure points in your face, in the eyebrows, around the jaw, temples etc.

Foot aches. Wear comfortable shoes. Not for nothing do in my experience bassists, who stand the most, always wear the most comfortable shoes.

Drugs. Just one word. Don't!

Adrenaline is the best and a natural drug supplied by your body. You do stuff well, it gets released. It may be an oversimplification, but all great masters that changed the world with their creative output, did it first with focus, talent and intense will. Drugs, if so, came second and have had a detrimental effect.

Mental fatigue, questions about the validity of one's way and one's self, and burn out are a serious problem, as we give it all. We share our soul, our accomplishments with the world and are measured against an immense catalogue. Nowadays you have to be able to play great, be a social media expert, produce all your stuff etc. What to do? Take one step at a time. Get the music together, and then everything else. Music can save your soul from over-everything. And the more you have to say on your instrument, the bigger the cushion that can absorb all the other distractions and issues.

Much still remains to be said about health. Please send all your questions and observations to me. I will answer and discuss them in videos. Just know that everyone that plays an instrument has problems they are fighting with because of that. Much of music is fueled by overcoming these problems.

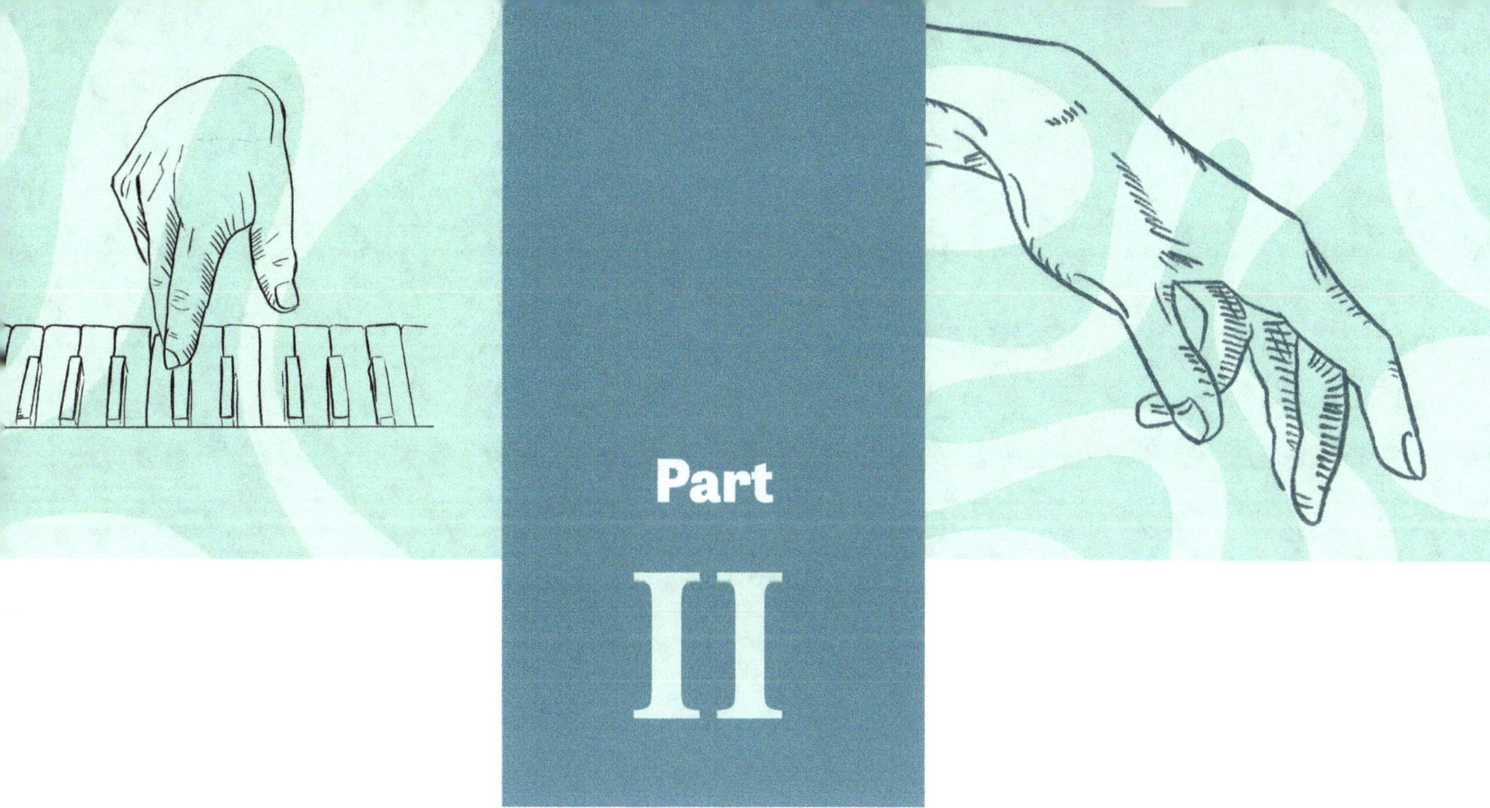

II

The Art of Practicing

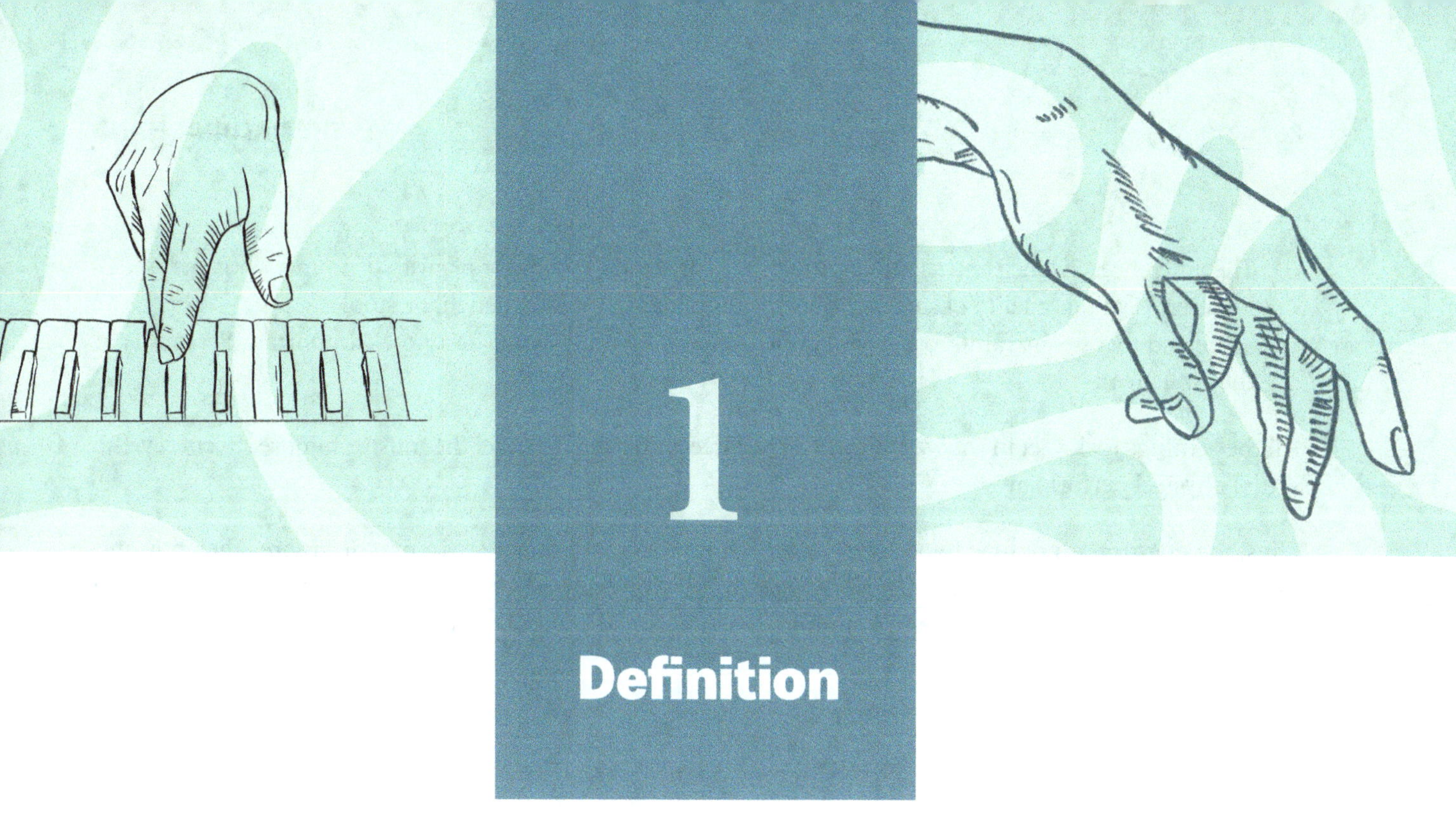

1

Definition

Practicing is the transfer of information from the conscious to the subconscious. Information may be facts like notes or any movement like playing.

Most playing and performing is governed by the subconscious.

The conscious mind has to maneuver the five senses' input and figure out what is necessary to focus on. What, at that moment, needs to be maximally focused on. We strive to be as much in the moment as possible. This helps reduce uncertainty and nervousness (see Chapter 6).

Concentration and focus help us maneuver all the conscious bits and maximize the outcome of the learned.

The subconscious is where the actual knowledge is stored, and it needs very conscious practicing to get there in order to have it readily available and play beautifully.

If this sounds a bit muddled and mysterious, here is a clarifying example. Most everyone has problems playing their best when showing up for a lesson. Sentences like "I played it so much better at home," "I did practice this a lot, but…" and so on are often heard. But why is this so? Because our conscious mind interferes with the learned, making it painfully obvious how much of the studied material has actually been absorbed and placed in the subconscious, and how much is not there yet.

What is the conscious dealing with?

- The lighting and ambiance
- The smell
- The temperature and humidity
- The sound in a different room

- The differences in touch and sound of a different instrument (mostly for pianists, drummers, organists, etc.)
- Different seating (quality of support, density and size of the chair, bench, or stool)
- Time and focus constraints, otherwise known as pressure (play your best now! "Important Person" is in the audience).

All these things really get in the way of our main concern to listen and feel the music or, more succinctly, the actual physical performance.

Thus, the question is not how to perform better but how to practice better. To practice more efficiently and thoroughly, leading to a deeper level of knowledge and command so that all the conscious nuances can be shed aside or used to advantage (e.g., communicating with the audience; see Chapter 7).

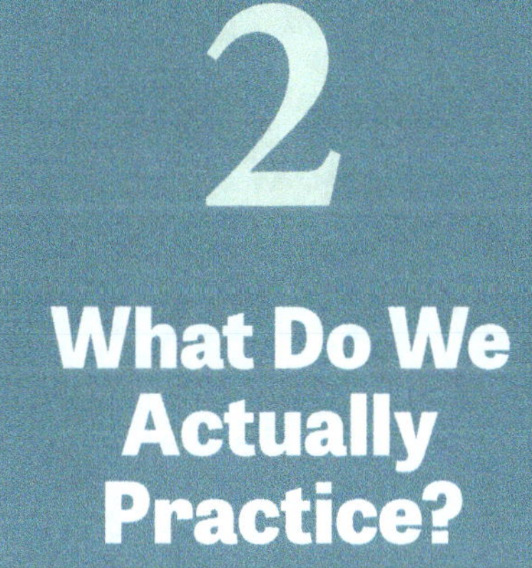

2

What Do We Actually Practice?

Music is a performance art and very physical. We train our mind, but just as importantly we need to train our body. If you don't have a physical, visceral reaction and feedback to what you play, the outcome will be not satisfying. Thus, we need to practice feel and physical placement. If you feel it internally, you should be able to physically manifest it externally.

"Feeling it" refers to a plethora of different sensations:

- Time: It starts with feeling the "time" in your playing, to feel the time throughout your body. "The time"—aka groove, beat, rhythm, meter, accents, and so on—refers to the tangible part of music. This is what our bodies should unite with.
- Arms: It also means feeling the movement of your arms, guiding the phrases with your upper body and arms.
- Foot: It also means feeling the time by stomping the foot, especially when playing jazz, Latin, pop, and so on. In classical music, this is rather frowned upon, but can be of great use during practice.
- Singing: The placement of a note when you sing. This refers to the placement in time and in your body.
- Breathing: Correct breathing helps all musicians, not just singers. It is advisable to breathe with the music, the phrases, and the subdivisions—most of the time this happens automatically, but, when you're stuck, check your breathing
- Coordination: The interaction with legs is of course especially important for a drummer, but it does not stop there. Pianist, harpists, organists—all have actual foot movements. But even all the other instrumentalists need to think about placement of the feet as part of the physical manifestation of the piece and groove they are playing.

Again, playing music is a physical manifestation, and you have to have a whole-body experience. Time is, and you manifest it through your playing. A groove has many layers but a common pulse. We are uniting with the pulse and dance with our playing on top of it, creating more layers that add to the whole.

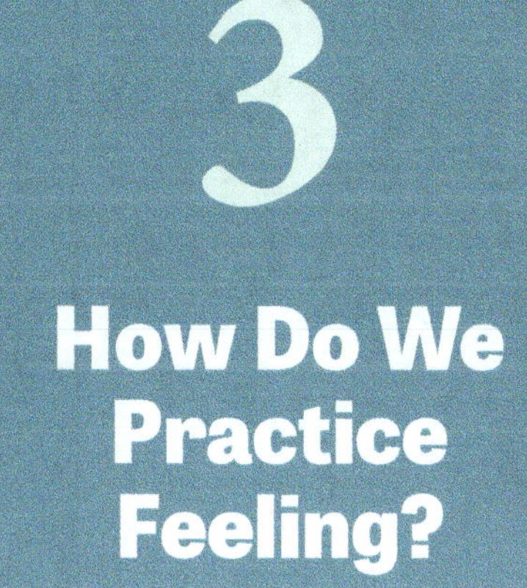

3

How Do We Practice Feeling?

Ah, the million-dollar question.

Here are the elements:

- Listening
- Singing
- Scatting (rhythmic singing less tonal)
- Playing your instrument slowly, often with eyes closed and always with ears open.[1]

When we are simply playing notes, even the correct ones, we are reducing practicing to a callisthenic exercise that is devoid of actual music—mind you, there is a place for this sort of practice, but it's a small place and shouldn't occupy any larger amount of time. The following will help you feel the music (it's an obvious list, but sometimes we forget).

- Play along with tunes
- Play along with sequences
- Play "along" with humans

Remember: Music is a language; we learn a language by imitating and feeling the sounds. All schools and programs fall short when focusing solely on the brain and the intellectual dance we do around music, which is aptly called Theory therefore.

---

[1] Many passages are hard to play slow and require to be played more rapidly. Often, the fingering, especially the arm movement, cannot be figured out properly until you actually play it at the right speed. Several Chopin exercises, pieces by Liszt, and elements of Latin playing come to mind.

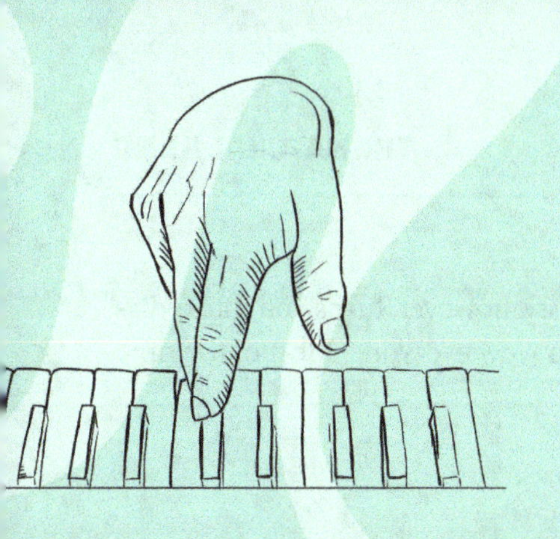

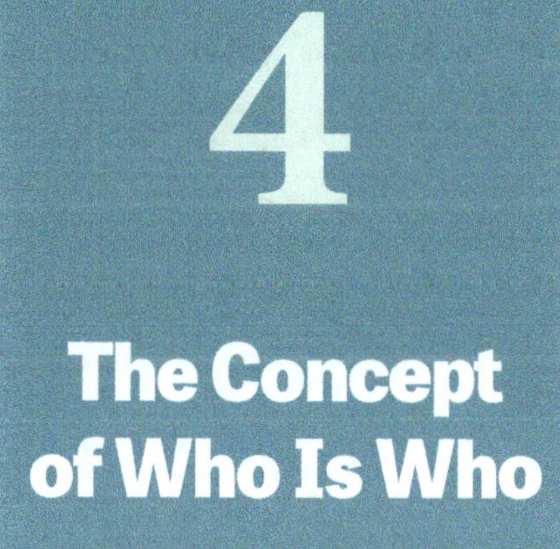

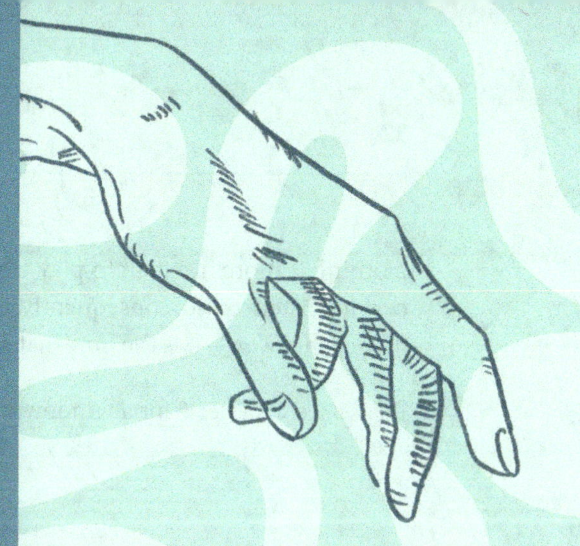

4

The Concept of Who Is Who

You are your own teacher.

Your teacher is a guide, but you have to make sure the daily steps are successful.

How to do that?

Set for yourself small, attainable goals—if you only learn and absorb one phrase a day it's enough, as long as you keep up the pace.

Be critical and detail oriented—you are the boss when practicing. You can act like one or accept mediocre success.

Listen to everything you play—arguably, the pianist* (*fill in your instrument) that you listen to the most in your life is yourself. Try to please yourself and please your own ears with the music you create.

Play to your own high standard of what you like to hear. And then make that the benchmark. It's all in the attitude toward your own self. Trust your abilities, your taste, and your achievements when playing. Self-scorn and depreciation is, although widely practiced, not helpful. Here's one I have been extremely guilty of—when someone, anyone, compliments you, take it and thank the person. You created a positive spark. At that moment, it doesn't matter that this was only half as good as you wanted to do, as you could have played if—it really doesn't matter. Someone else was touched, so don't take that away from them by trying to be cooler than you really are.

Honesty to when it sounds right and when it feels right are quintessential to a great outcome.

Nothing is more fun than to play what you know and wow yourself. Honesty, however, turns you into a discerning listener and, consequently, a better player with many more ways to wow everyone. Most of the time it's not the *what*—it is the *how* that we need to figure out.

Please see Chapter 8 for a rundown of time management and rehearsal ideas.

5

The Steps—A Collection of Tidbits and Aphorisms

Below steps are all part of a greater truth, which defines and redefines itself the more advanced you become (truth may be seen as the daily personal view and convictions on the subject of music). All the same, below principles will hold true, no matter the level. You can read through these steps or explore each one of them separately. The latter approach will probably yield more success. I have tried all these things myself and with my students, and swear by each of them.

A. Defining Practice

First off, practice is the hardest thing in any daily schedule. It is work. It can be fun.

- If you feel exhausted in a good way afterwards, it means you have done something right.
- Have goals—Only when you know what you want to accomplish can you get there quickly.
- Small increments—Learn things one phrase at a time.
- Learn backwards, especially longer pieces—This is a concept that I learned from classical teachers. Every time I had my students practice like that, no matter the level, they played better and learned more thoroughly. And their performance had more confidence.
- Learn the lyrics—Please learn the lyrics and sing them. Then figure out what's your key and learn the song there. We don't have to be all singers, but we need to play a melody knowing what it's about. When listening I can tell immediately who knows the lyrics and who doesn't in the way they phrase the melody.
- Sing everything! The melody, the chords, the bass line, the groove, an improvisation—it really helps.

- Play no wrong notes. Yes, this may sound like a dream or a joke, but it is quite possible if you play slowly enough. This is an intense time saver and builds accuracy and, especially, confidence.
- Speed comes from knowledge—The more thoroughly you know something, the easier it is to execute at any tempo.

B. Jazz-related steps

- A scale is a chord is a harmony. Paraphrasing Gertrude Stein, it means that a specific sound is formed by more than one element or multiple elements that in turn are sides of the same coin. As pianists we have the amazing chance to enjoy that cohesion with the left-hand chording while the right is soloing. Ideally, they agree unless chosen otherwise.
- Melodies have directions—your improvisation should, too. A cool way to practice this is to make up words and create a melody for them. Hi, my name is Jim, could be:

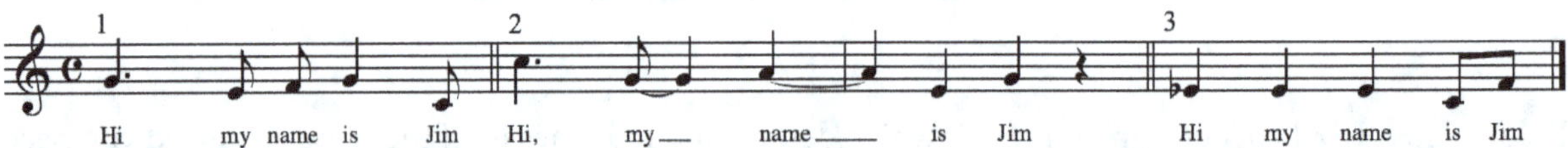

- A strong melody is always stronger than harmony, because our linear and melodic perception far out-weighs everything else.
- Never forget exploration—in exploration, there are no wrong notes, and different resolutions might improve the exploration.
- A good melody survives most treatments. Go ahead, arrange, and re-harmonize to your heart's content. Every approach to a standard is good as long as it gets you closer to your own sound. Mind you, sometimes treatments of known songs are best reserved for one's own ears or later on for exploring with friends. It's okay to quickly discard them.
- Patterns are great. Practice them, internalize them, and immediately apply them to all the tunes you like to play. Improvisation is made up mostly of stuff you know. Practice lots of great stuff, so your improvisation feels more grounded.
- Learn a tune a week (minimum). When I say learn, I mean putting in efforts to develop the command to play it in several keys, different tempos, knowing the lyrics, and so on.
- Create your own real book. This is a collection of standards or tunes you like to learn. I have my students start their own tune book, where new songs are added. If you can sit down and write out a tune, you know it. Then add analysis, great recordings of it, who wrote it when, for what, in which key—lots of little things can end up on that tune page that will help you to engrain them in your memory and play the composition with more authority.
- Every day: Singing and listening and transcribing and writing—everyday just a few minutes to hours of this. Always work on something in your head.

- Learn and compose contrafacts (new melody on standard changes). That's a great way to learn and create melodic integrity.
- Learn drums, no matter your instrument, and percussion, too. You really should be able to play a shaker and groove with it. For any Latin and African music it is essential to know the governing patterns.
- Learn piano, no matter your instrument. There is no better way to understand music than through the piano. It's all there staring at you. You don't have to be able to play a gig on it, but it's a cool goal.
- Learn a wind instrument, no matter your instrument. To learn how to phrase when you actually deal with breath as a form of survival has no substitute. Again, it's more about the principle than to become great at it, which, of course, doesn't hurt either.

C. Aphorisms

I. FINGERING

Fingering should be considered along the principles of the natural hand: No overly held tension, fluidity is key, and use the thumb to its maximum efficiency.

II. THE CUBE

Any music has to be understood on several levels. Take the time and see any given piece as a multisided cube. There are many sides and facets that may be discovered on any one item, one piece of music. They might be physically in your body; more cerebrally in your head, as in theory and facts; and then the real music, which is a combination of both, including form, melodies, lyrics, harmonies, and their rhythmical impetus.

III. ANTICIPATION

Always listen and feel ahead. Music is anticipatory. We are always in motion toward the end. Imagine a train in which you can go back and forth, but as soon as you get off, especially while moving, you're out of the piece. The back and forth, the slowing down or speeding up is called agogic and rubato, which is essential to great music. However, getting off the pulse means going back to the drawing board and practice.

IV. SLOW, SLOWER

Play slower than you feel and think you can do. Go for accuracy over speed at first. Play deliberately with a clear sense of knowing what to achieve. As stated before, try to play without any mistake, that way you never have to fix it!

V. ACCURACY

Know what to listen for when you practice. Be sure of the sound and sound quality and how it relates to the articulation.

VI. ALWAYS WITH A GROOVE/RHYTHM/PULSE/FLOW

By now this is rather repetitive, but I can't state if often enough: Music is a physical manifestation and needs to be felt from the ground up; no matter the style or the rhythm.

VII. BALANCE

Every movement has a counter movement. Watch a drummer hit a strong hit, and you'll see the rebound afterwards. In piano, the action rebounds. A bow has a balance and rebounds and so on.

Motion is transformed into to sound waves. Body waves and motion are transformed into sound waves. When you play something very intense you have to have space afterwards to create balance.

VIII. FORETHOUGHT

How do I need to practice to achieve the goal? How does the phrase manifest physically in me?

In order to play a phrase well, transpose it, change it rhythmically, play it with both hands, and so on. The more you challenge your mind beyond the actual phrase, the more the phrase will fall in place. Why did I call this forethought? Because sometimes we need to figure out the how, through variations of the problem, and that requires reflection.

IX. GUIDES

The ear and the voice are great guides. Follow their lead. There are innate maestros in you and your ear and your voice are the guides to discovering them.

X. REPETITION

Play it 5 times perfectly!

As suggested by a brilliant master of the piano, Mykola Suk, five times is the way. Take five toothpicks. After each instance move one over. When you make a mistake or even the slightest hesitation go back. This serves as indicator and also creates a little brake between instances, ensuring it doesn't become mechanical.

XI. EXAMPLES

1. Here's a simple bass groove (used in Bossa, Samba, etc.) to demonstrate feeling it in your body.

Groove example

2. A simple scale to demonstrate the importance and action of the thumb.

Scale

What is a scale? It's an extended, fairly uniform, melody. This means we have to experience the whole of it from start to finish. We listen to each note, how it blends and forms a string of pearls if you will. Ideally, we are able to play it uniformly, up and down. Try these:

- Sing along, no matter the octave.
- Breathe along in time or use one long breath.
- Listen and feel ahead. Phrases need to be felt from the beginning to end - one arch.

3. The famous Hanon number #1

Hanon

As soon as one understands both up and down patterns, the only problem is the turnaround at the top. We should listen to the implied scalar melodies. We need to anticipate the top and bottom and the turnaround.

6

On Being Nervous

Levels of nervousness include the following:

A. Exhilarating and focusing—performance enhancing
B. Creating doubt and double-guessing
C. Stopping to listen and getting stuck in the moment
D. Losing your place—memory slips—shaking hands and voice

Above levels are very crude, and the many levels of nervousness are equal to the amount of people being nervous. Everyone gets nervous. Everyone doubts. Everyone needs affirmation.

Nervousness, in its basic form, is an anxiousness created by the inability to stay in the moment. What does that mean? We are anxious about the upcoming event so that we are losing our grip on the actual timeline. Our mind is jumping around and trying to anticipate. Suddenly time is not objective, but seems to have a life of its own. "This takes forever" "What already?" "I can't wait to..." A famous and very common pattern is that the student speeds up through a challenging passage. Somehow, we just want to get done with it.

The worst is during a performance, when we lose the ability to feel and listen ahead, lose the most-needed awareness to anticipate. That may be anticipating the phrase, the dynamic, the groove, most obviously anticipating the correct notes, fingerings, and so on.

Our hearing seems disjunctive, and the timeline is slipping. Please forgive me in advance, but I believe in my heart that all levels of nervousness are conquerable. How? We need to steady our mind with the best-focused practice. We have to allow ourselves a moment of joy and pride over even the most mundane accomplishments. Like weathering a storm, the fundamentals are key and the constant lookout on how to perfect and improve one's performance is broken down into many, many steps. Is it a daunting task? Intense and full of labor yes, but not daunting. The thought of giving up or not trying seems much worse to me.

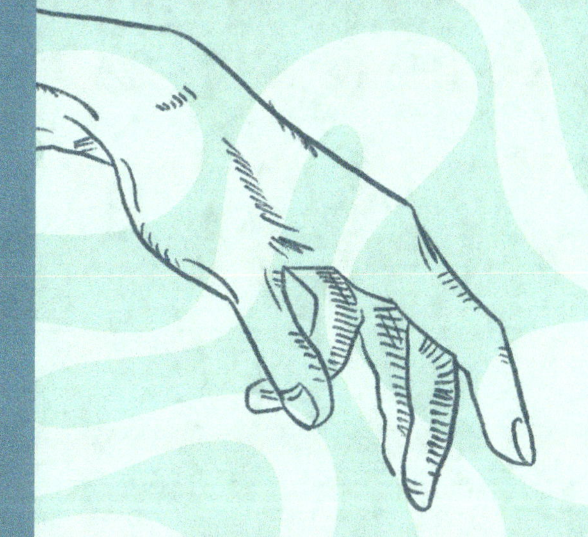

7

Communicat-ing with the Audience

Why do we need to communicate? Isn't it enough to play great? Isn't that a form of communication?

Well, yes, but with the advent of every aspect of life being recorded and much of it being visible immediately, we all need to communicate better. Today, most people tend to listen more with their eyes than with their ears and that general mindset is not much different when watching (!) a live event. Social media, TedTalks, YouTube, all have upped the ante of self-promotion. Thus, when you present a show or concert today, the audience expects to be entertained in word and sound. Even most classical conductors nowadays show of their witty side and create a whole new level of approachable as opposed to mystical and revered maestros and maestras of the classical and jazz world of the yesteryear.

Here is a caveat—the transition from being immersed in the music and then talking in a relaxed and engaging manner to the audience is tough. You are stepping out from one bubble into another one and back. It takes practice. It helped me, to think of it as switching hats. What seems to work really well is to literally draw your audience into your bubble on stage, akin to creating a living-room atmosphere. Again, that does not happen from one day to the next, but it is something necessary to develop as performer now. Enjoy talking about what moves you. The audience will thank you with applause and more.

However, no matter how good the communication with your audience is, your playing should always be much more advanced!

Communicating while playing.

When we perform we need to communicate non verbally. It boils down to being involved as energeticlly as possible. Learn from other performers and see what sticks with you. Observation and a keen eye for even the smallest details are needed.

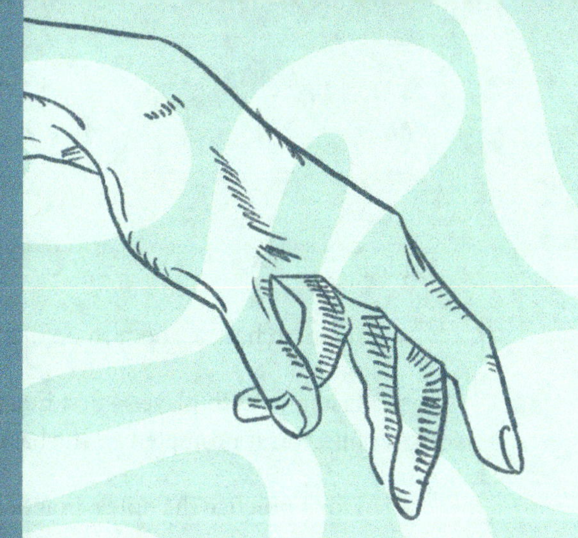

8

Time Management—How to Focus

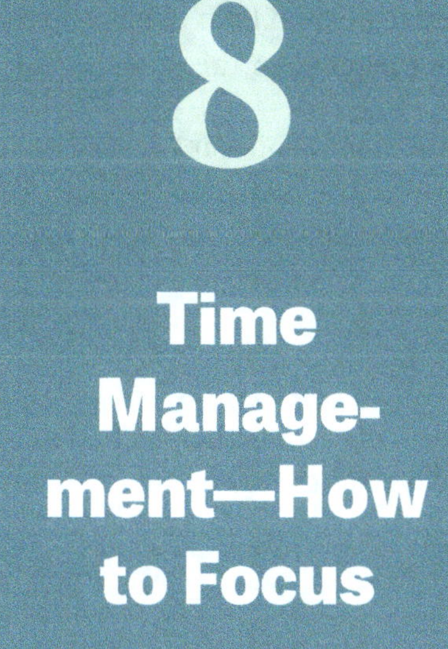

In the definition "to manage one's time" immediately the obvious is shown. We need to step out of the artistic side and become more accountant-like. But be a knowing accountant who knows yourself and your own strengths and weaknesses.

1. Short sessions—Break practice down to short manageable goals

Usually, my focus starts waning after 15 to 20 minutes. Yes, I have practiced for 7 and 8 hours before, but the real focus when I absorb new stuff is parceled into fairly short periods. Figure out what you can accomplish in 15 minutes. Set a timer and start practicing, and every 15 minutes take stock. In a couple of days, it will be very obvious where your strengths and lengths of focus lay.

A goal is the steppingstone to success.

2. Think in musical phrases—Take these and make them your goals

How to start? With a tie. Whatever is under a tie is a phrase. Wherever there's a rest, breathe and see if the next phrase should be practiced together.

3. Listening to recordings is practice!

That's a big one.

As a musician listening is the most important aspect we need to get together. Not only ear training but training how to listen and what to listen for.

Ideas:

- In an orchestra, zoom in on one instrument.

  Listen to each player—first independently and then in a group focus. Why does the drummer play this fill? Was it prompted by the bass or the piano or the soloist?

- Don't practice the notes; practice the sound you want to create

  For example, a Bebop line is made into Bebop by the right accents. The phrasing and conviction create the sound.

- Slowly in and slowly out

  Yehudi Menuhin coined this priceless phrase and helped to demonstrate it with a pointing finger to one ear and out the other. Practice slowly and it sticks better.

- Practice from the end

  As said before, it's great to know where you're musically going and be able to do so with conviction.

- Figure out the trouble spot(s)

  Isn't that self-understood? Well, yes and no. It obviously makes sense, but to actually practice the exact trouble spot and then incorporate it bit by bit in the neighboring material is not always done. Usually it occurs on a turnaround, a repeat or connecting idea, when the composer spices things up to create intensity, when the action gets a little more intense, or it is time to wrap things up.

Each phrase deserves special ways of going about it.

This is where I once again encourage you to write to me so we can discuss specific problems and may later incorporate them into the next edition.

9

The Other Problems

A. Inaccurate Hearing

Hearing is the most important faculty for all musicians.

In jazz, we all improvise together along a defined speed and within a defined form. Every player has instrument-specific patterns and figures, phrases that will overlap and interlock with the other players.

We need to be aware of several different layers:

Rhythmic
Melodic
Harmonic

Within all three are licks, melodies, and phrases that are known and from which we can draw.

The next step is awareness of the form and the subdivisions. Hearing and feeling ahead is very important. When does it go to the bridge and how do I play in it? How do I anticipate the coming section?

So how to improve one's hearing? Make it a priority! Listening should be as much of daily practice as everything else. For example, listen to a recording many times over, but always focus on a different element and instrument <u>all the way through</u>.

B. Lack of Focus

Lack of focus is probably a most common problem and not just in music.

The remedy? Increments. Focus is a mental discipline that almost works like a muscle. It needs to be trained. Start by playing five notes in a row with the exact same touch, length, and loudness. Go through all the keys and lengthen the phrase. Now apply this state of concentration and focus to everything else.

Another way how to increase focus is physical exercise and meditation.

C. Lack of Discipline

Discipline goes hand in hand with self-worth.

If you don't believe in your playing and your craft, you have less motivation to be disciplined. Far from wanting to give psychiatric advice, please let me tell you that everyone who plays an instrument is an important part for society at large. You create positive energy and that's a worthwhile goal.

D. Lack of Social Skills

This is a touchy subject, but I believe if music can teach you one thing, then it is to be humble.

The sea of music is seemingly endless, and we can traverse it our whole life. We meet people who realize that and are humbled by this fact, and we meet people who are frustrated by the very same fact. It's good to stay on the humble side. It makes life more enjoyable.

There is always another player who knows more, plays faster, has more engagements, and so on.

And to take it to the professional level, there's always one who is on time, wears the right clothes, knows the right tunes, and plays the gig (to play the gig means to make everyone on the bandstand feel comfortable). It's not the one who knows the most, but the one that's most integrative!). And mind you, a solo piano gig at a wedding and an orchestra concert at Carnegie Hall are still two sides of the same coin. Social skills are not just the way you say hello, but the way you present yourself to the rest of the world.

I suggest reading a diverse range of books and covering many a classic. Perspective and ways to cope with life and everything are right there.

E. Lack of Self-confidence

See discipline. Discipline can teach us self-worth. Whenever one accomplishes something through own efforts, it raises the spirit.

One of the worst things many of us do is that we find it necessary to diminish our efforts in order to be cool. While it's cool to be humble, it's nonsensical to not appreciate yourself.

How to build up self-confidence is to take every task seriously and complete it step by step. The most brilliant minds have taken this approach since they were little, which accounts for much of their brilliance!

Said **Michelangelo**: *If people knew how hard I worked to get my mastery, it wouldn't seem so wonderful at all!*

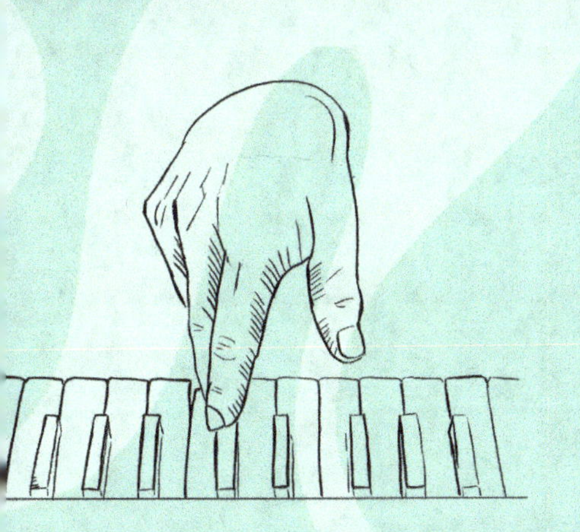

10

Closing and Looking Ahead

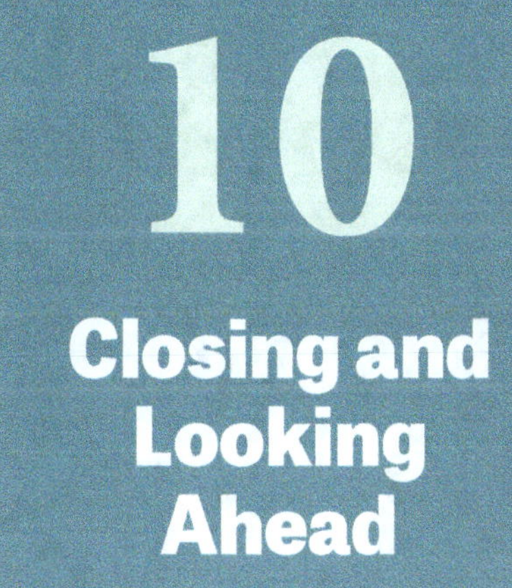

Now that we're at the end of the first volume, thank you for your patience following along.

There are a lot of concepts in here, and I am looking forward to all your questions and comments and will elaborate on each point in writing and video on my patreon site and in personal emails and/or video calls or lessons. And there's always a second edition!

I can't wait to bring out the new volumes for all the other instrument groups as well.

Please do yourself proud and become a mindful monster musician. Mindfulness is a trendy concept, but in music, it has lived as long as we play. Without listening it's all a sham.

Happy Practicing

Uli

Henderson, Nevada
Spring of 2023

*Patreon-site is patreon.com/ulimusic

Uli Geissendoerfer

German-American pianist, composer, producer and educator, Uli Geissendoerfer has been living and working in the US since 1987. In 2009 he moved from his spiritual home New York as musical director for Cirque du Soleil's Viva Elvis production to Las Vegas. While teaching at UNLV (invited by Dave Loeb), his Latin ensemble won six Downbeat awards including 1st place in 2015. In 2011 he initiated a lecture series at the University bringing in over 50 guest artists since. He founded the Jazz Club at the Dispensary Lounge in 2012 (winning *Best of Las Vegas*), which revived the Las Vegas Jazz scene and featured luminaries such as Wynton Marsalis, Brandon Fields, Sam Most, Rick Margitza, Dick Griffin, Scott Henderson, Danny Gottlieb, George Garzone and many more, that performed there with his Trio and Quartet. In 2021 he started a new club, The Gambit.

His first Vegas production "Colors", 2012, featured a great quintet with Charles McNeal, Pascale Elia, Derek Jones and Ryan Rose. The opening tune of album "3-41" won 1st place in the 13th IMA awards. In the Fall of 2017, he joined the new Jazz Program at the Nevada School of the Arts and founded *Vegas Records*, promoting the local jazz scene and music from UNLV's Jazz department (now 23 releases). In 2018 he received the part-time-teacher-of the-year award from the Fine Arts department at UNLV.

His current projects the *Uli Geissendoerfer Trio*, backbone of the Jazz Club, with their CD *"Long Way Home"*, the *"Beregovski Suite"*, a duo with the fabulous, award winning violin virtuoso Alicia Svigals and his European Quartet featuring Pascale Elia. His new endeavors as author saw a Jazz History text book written with Robert Shipley for Kendall Hunt Publishing and a five part series "The Natural Hand & The Art of Practicing" with the first volume published by Innovative Ink in your hands.

Two new albums a Duo and a Quartet with Julian Tanaka came out this year on Vegas Records. He is also producing several singers including Ray Brown Jr., Michelle Johnson, Linda Woodson, check out her fabulous album *Come A Little Closer*, and others.

He has worked with, among others, William Cepeda (Grammy nomination), Groove Collective, Giovanni Hidalgo, Blood Sweat & Tears, Leslie Uggams, Cirque du Soleil, Ute Lemper, David Cassidy, Tito Puente, several Symphonies, the Connecticut Opera and a bevy of Jazz greats and African Artists.

Website:
www.ulimusic.com

Discography:
https://uligeissendoerfer.bandcamp.com/

I
Appendix

Study Books for Piano Technique

Mechanics:
Carl Czerny—Op. 299 School of Velocity Op. 740—The Art of Finger Dexterity.

Moritz Mozskowski—15 Etudes de Virtuosite, Op. 72 (#9 is great for octave technique).

Alfred Cortot—Rational-Principles-of-Pianoforte-Technique-1928.

The brilliant pianist Cortot knocked it out of the park with this. In his brilliant treatise almost all technical issues are covered. The appendix with the listing of classical pieces and their relative difficulty and technical focus alone is amazing.

Fredric Chopin—Etudes Op. 10 and Op. 25.
If you never study anything but Chopin, you'll be fine.

Bela Bartok—Mikrokosmos Vol. 1 to 6 (as much hated as loved, these are great practice pieces).

Brahms—51 Exercises
Several of these are a must.

Clare Fischer—Harmonic Exercises for Piano
Probably inspired by Czerny's Toccata

Bach—The Well-Tempered Clavier I and II

Nothing puts your fingers together like this—great music and technical challenges combined. Said my late piano teacher Radosevic:
It's a good day, when it starts with Bach.

Hanon—The Virtuoso Pianist
Learn and transpose exercises # 1 and #2 to all keys.

II

Appendix

The Natural Hand—Next Volumes

Vol. II String Instruments
     Violin, viola, cello, bass acoustic, bass electric

Vol. III Wind Instruments
     A. Brass—trumpet, trombone, French horn,
     B. Wood—saxophones, flute, clarinet, oboe, English horn, bassoon

Vol. IV Drums and Percussion
     A. Sticks—drum set
     B. Mallets—Vibes, Marimba, glockenspiel
     C. Hand percussion—congas, Djembe, bata, barilles

Vol. V The Voice
     A. Classical
     B. Jazz
     C. Pop